A+ books

Nature Starts

WHOSE EGG Is This?

by Lisa J. Amstutz

Content Consultant:
Bernd Heinrich, PhD
Department of Biology
University of Vermont

CAPSTONE PRESS
a capstone imprint

A+ Books are published by Capstone Press,
1710 Roe Crest Drive, North Mankato, Minnesota 56003.
www.capstonepub.com

Books published by Capstone Press are manufactured with paper
containing at least 10 percent post-consumer waste.

Library of Congress Cataloging-in-Publication Data
Amstutz, Lisa J.
  Whose egg is this? / by Lisa J. Amstutz.
    p. cm.—(A+ Books. Nature starts)
  Includes bibliographical references.
  Summary: "Simple text and full-color photos ask multiple-choice questions about which animal laid
each egg"—Provided by publisher.
  ISBN 978-1-4296-7554-3 (library binding) – ISBN 978-1-4296-7854-4 (paperback)
  1. Eggshells—Juvenile literature. I. Title. II. Series.
SF490.3.A67 2012
591.4'68—dc23   2011027266

Credits

Katy Kudela, editor; Juliette Peters, designer; Marcie Spence, media researcher;
    Laura Manthe, production specialist

Photo Credits

Alamy: All Canada Photos, 13 (bottom left), 28 (bottom middle), Brandon Cole Marine Photography, 1,
24, JTB Photo Communications, Inc., 27 (bottom left), 29 (bottom right), Mark Conlin, 21 (bottom right),
29 (top right), Natural Visions, 20, Naturepix, 10, Papilio, cover (left), 8; Corbis: Jeffrey L. Rotman, 22,
Reinhard Dirscherl/Visuals Unlimited, 18; iStockphoto: 33karen33, 21 (top right), DanSchmitt, 25 (top left), 29
(bottom middle), kawisign, 27 (top right); Photo Researchers, Inc.: Paul Whitten, 14; Reproduced by permission
from Platypus (Fourth Edition), Copyright Tom Grant and Dominic Fanning 2007, Published by CSIR, 26;
Shutterstock: Alena Brozova, 3, Alvaro Pantoja, 19 (bottom right), Andy Z., 19 (bottom left), 29 (top middle),
artcasta, 15 (bottom left), Brian J. Abela, 21 (bottom left), Bronwen Sexton, 6, Dhoxax, 19 (top right), Dr. Morley
Read, 17 (bottom left), Ellie Mae, 17 (top left), 29 (top left), erllre74, 15 (top right), 28 (bottom right), Evocation
Images, 23 (bottom right), Gert Johannes Jacobus Very, 11 (bottom left), Heidi Schneider, 13 (bottom right),
holbox, 21 (top left), Inna_77, 4, irin-k, 17 (top right), Jacinta, 15 (top left), James Laurie, cover (middle right),
9 (bottom left), 28 (top right), Jan Martin Will, 7 (top right), javarman, cover (top right), 9 (top left), Johan
Swanepoel, 11 (top right), 28 (bottom left), Jurie Maree, 23 (top right), 29 (bottom left), kentoh, 7 (bottom left),
Luis Fernando Curci Chavier, 25 (bottom left), Luis Marquez, cover (bottom right), 9 (bottom right), Malota,
27 (top left), Marek R. Swadzba, 27 (bottom right), Martha Marks, 7 (top left), 28 (top left), nene, cover
(design element), Nikita Tiunov, 23 (bottom left), Pavel K, cover (design element), Peter Betts, 11 (bottom right),
photobypiers, 25 (bottom right), Reinhold Leitner, 11 (top left), Roman & Olexandra, 23 (top left), 25 (top right),
Ron Rowan Photography, 16, Rusty Dodson, 7, (bottom right), Ryan Arnaudin, 19 (top left), siloto, 13 (top right),
Splash, 5, Stefan Fierros, 12, Tiago Jorge da Silva Estima, cover (middle right), 9 (top right), Trevor Kelly, 30,
Triff, 17 (bottom right), ULKASTUDIO, 15 (bottom right), Victor Shova, 13 (top left)

Note to Parents, Teachers, and Librarians

This Nature Starts book uses full color photographs and a nonfiction format to introduce the
concept of animal life cycles. *Whose Egg Is This?* is designed to be read aloud to a pre-reader
or to be read independently by an early reader. Photographs help listeners and early readers
understand the text and concepts discussed. The book encourages further learning by including
the following sections: Glossary, Read More, and Internet Sites. Early readers may need assistance
using these features.

Printed in the United States of America in North Mankato, Minnesota.
102011   006405CGS12

THE INCREDIBLE EGG

An egg is the start of a new baby animal. Until the baby hatches, the egg holds everything the animal needs to grow. The yolk feeds the baby. The egg white keeps the yolk safe. A membrane lets water and air go in and out. Some eggs have hard shells to keep them safe.

Eggs come in different colors, shapes, and sizes. Eggs can be hard or soft. They can be smooth or rough.

Eggs might hatch in a nest. They might hatch in a pond. Some eggs hatch with a little help from their parents.

Can you guess which animal laid these eggs?

Keep reading and make your best guess! You can find the correct answers on pages 28 and 29.

These blue eggs rest high in a tree in a nest of twigs and grass. A mother with reddish-orange chest feathers keeps the eggs warm. Once the babies hatch, she will feed them worms.

WHOSE EGGS ARE THESE?

ROBIN

PENGUIN

BAT

SNAKE

Hint! You know spring is near when you spot one of these in your yard!

Under a milkweed leaf, a tiny egg waits. In 10 days, a striped caterpillar will crawl out. It will munch on milkweed leaves. Soon it will turn into a pupa. Then it will become an adult with orange and black wings.

WHOSE EGG IS THIS?

CRAB

TIGER

MONARCH BUTTERFLY

ORIOLE

Hint! Before the snow flies, this animal heads south. It flies to warmer weather. In spring, its children or grandchildren will travel back home.

These cream-colored eggs are the biggest of all eggs. Their mother and father take turns sitting on them. These giant eggs stay warm in a nest hole in the sand.

WHOSE EGGS ARE THESE?

GIANT
TORTOISE

OSTRICH

CROCODILE

ELEPHANT

Hint !

The parents of this baby are almost
8 feet (2.4 meters) tall. They can't fly.
But they sure can run fast!

11

This soft, jelly-like glob has thousands of tiny black eggs inside. The babies will hatch in a pond. They will live in the water until their legs grow.

WHOSE EGGS ARE THESE?

12

HERMIT CRAB

DUCK

FROG

GOLDFISH

 Hint! As an adult, this animal has lungs. It also breathes through its skin.

These eggs sit in a rotten log or under a rock. The babies inside use a special egg tooth to break through their shells. They peek out for awhile then slither away.

WHOSE EGGS ARE THESE?

WORM

SNAKE

SNAIL

TURTLE

Hint !

Can you smell with your tongue? This animal can. Flicking it in and out brings smells to an organ in its mouth.

15

This silk sac holds 100 tiny eggs. The babies hatch inside the sac. When it gets warm outside, they come out. Then they spin silk parachutes and float away.

WHOSE EGGS ARE THESE?

16

SPIDER

LADYBUG

CENTIPEDE

BEE

 Hint! Each baby has eight legs and eight eyes.

They look like ping-pong balls, but these eggs are soft. Their mother buried them in a sandy beach. When the babies hatch, they will rush to the ocean and swim away.

WHOSE EGGS ARE THESE?

ALLIGATOR

SEAGULL

SEA TURTLE

STARFISH

Hint **!** A tough, bony shell helps keep this animal safe.

19

A strong mother fought her way upstream to lay these pink eggs. She swished her tail to dig a gravel nest for them. When the babies hatch, they will hide in the gravel until they are bigger. Later they will swim to the ocean.

WHOSE EGGS ARE THESE?

TUNA

MANATEE

DOLPHIN

SALMON

Hint!

These animals spend most of their lives in the ocean. When they swim to fresh water to lay eggs, they change color.

This mother glued thousands of eggs to her tail. When the babies are ready to hatch, she shakes them out. Each baby is only the size of a grain of rice.

WHOSE EGGS ARE THESE?

STINGRAY

LOBSTER

SHRIMP

SEA HORSE

 Hint ! This animal catches food with its sharp claws. Its home is the ocean floor.

Thousands of these tiny eggs hang like party streamers in a cave. Their mother guards them. When they hatch, the babies will float away.

WHOSE EGGS ARE THESE?

OCTOPUS

EEL

CLOWN FISH

JELLYFISH

Hint This animal has eight arms but no legs.
If danger is near, it changes colors to hide.

This egg is less than 1 inch (2.5 centimeters) long. A furry mother laid this egg deep in a burrow. After the baby hatches, it will snuggle with its mother and drink her milk. This baby's snout looks like a duck's bill.

WHOSE EGG IS THIS?

mm

cm 0 1 2 3

GOOSE

BEAVER

PLATYPUS

SALAMANDER

 Hint

Only two kinds of mammals lay eggs.
Both of these mammals live in Australia.

Guess Who?

Did you guess to whom all the eggs belong? Check out the answer key to find out if you were correct.

PAGES 6-7

Did you pick the **ROBIN**? If you did, you are correct! In spring, a female robin builds a nest and lays blue eggs. Up to four chicks hatch in one nest.

PAGES 8-9

A **MONARCH BUTTERFLY** lays her eggs on milkweed leaves. When the caterpillars hatch, they don't have to look for food. They munch on the milkweed leaves.

PAGES 10-11

These giant eggs belong to the **OSTRICH**, the world's largest bird. Females lay up to 10 eggs at a time.

PAGES 12-13

Hundreds of tadpoles will hatch from these slimy eggs. The tadpoles will grow legs and turn into adult **WOOD FROGS**.

PAGES 14-15

A female **CORN SNAKE** laid these eggs. Not all snakes lay eggs. Some give birth to live young.

28

PAGES 16-17

PAGES 18-19

PAGES 20-21

YELLOW GARDEN SPIDERS will hatch inside this sac. The spiderlings leave the sac when they can walk and spin silk.

The owner of these round eggs is a **SEA TURTLE**. Female sea turtles return to the beach where they were born to lay eggs.

A female **SOCKEYE SALMON** laid these eggs. Adults swim thousands of miles to spawn. They travel from the ocean back to the lake or stream where they were born.

PAGES 22-23

PAGES 24-25

PAGES 26-27

To keep her eggs safe, a **LOBSTER** sticks them to her tail. It can take up to 11 months before the babies hatch.

These tiny eggs came from a female **OCTOPUS**. When the babies hatch, they will float near the water's surface for a few weeks.

Did you guess the last answer? This leathery egg belongs to a mother **PLATYPUS**. The other mammal that lays eggs is the echidna.

Eggs are fun to look at. But eggs break easily. If you find a wild animal's egg, remember not to touch it. That way you will not hurt the growing animal inside.

Glossary

burrow—a tunnel or hole in the ground made or used by an animal

egg tooth—a sharp bump on top of an animal's nose or beak, used to break out of an egg

hatch—to break out of an egg

mammal—a warm-blooded animal that breathes air; mammals have hair or fur; female mammals feed milk to their young

membrane—a thin covering around the inside of an egg

pupa—a hard casing with an animal inside; the animal is changing from a larva to an adult

shell—a hard outer covering

silk—long, thin threads that stick together making an egg sac

spawn—to lay eggs

yolk—a yellow sac inside an egg, full of food for the unhatched animal

Read More

Baines, Rebecca. *What's In That Egg?: A Book about Life Cycles.* A Zigzag Book. Washington, D.C.: National Geographic, 2009.

Kenney, Karen Latchana. *Who Lays Eggs?* Our Animal World. Mankato, Minn.: Amicus, 2011.

Singer, Marilyn. *Eggs.* New York: Holiday House, 2008.

Internet Sites

FactHound offers a safe, fun way to find Internet sites related to this book. All of the sites on FactHound have been researched by our staff.

Here's all you do:

Visit *www.facthound.com*

Type in this code: 9781429675543

Check out projects, games and lots more at
www.capstonekids.com